NATURAL DISASTERS

by Madeline Nixon

Kaleidoscope
Minneapolis, MN

BIGFOOT BOOKS

The Quest for Discovery Never Ends

··

This edition first published in 2024 by Kaleidoscope Publishing, Inc.

For information regarding permission, write to Kaleidoscope Publishing, Inc.
6012 Blue Circle Drive
Minnetonka, MN 55343

Library of Congress Control Number
2023937031

ISBN
978-1-64519-739-3 (library bound)
978-1-64519-787-4 (ebook)

Printed in the United States of America.

FIND ME IF YOU CAN!

Bigfoot lurks within one of the images in this book. It's up to you to find him!

TABLE OF
CONTENTS

Chapter 1

WHITEOUT

The snow fell. And fell. And fell some more. It kept snowing until the **snowbanks** were 10 feet (3 m) tall.

Farah and her brother Ali had just read *The Chronicles of Narnia*. They thought all this snow looked just like that. But it wasn't a witch causing all the snow. It was a blizzard.

"Did I ever tell you about the blizzard I went through in Tennessee?" Farah and Ali's dad asked. The two shook their heads. They had never heard this story. "It was a lot like this. But even more snow. Can you believe that?"

"Whoa!" Farah said.

"Tell us more!" Ali said.

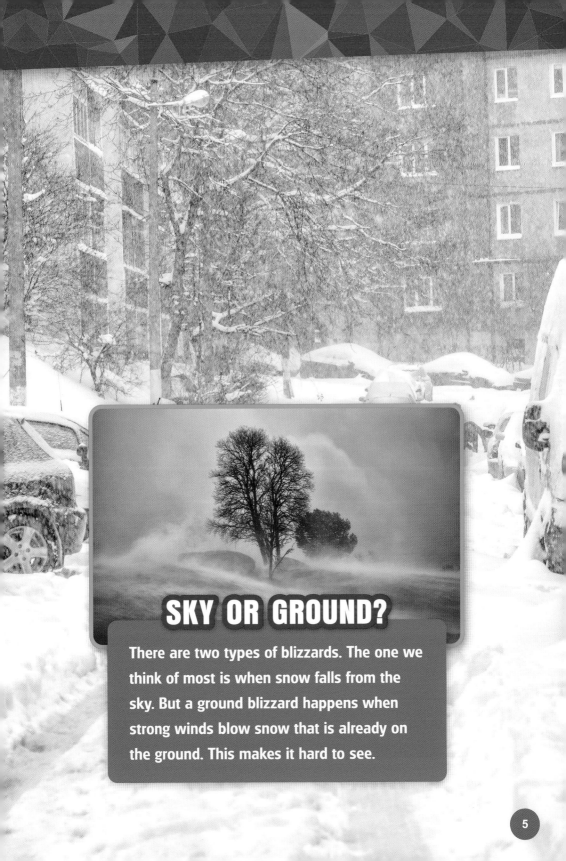

SKY OR GROUND?

There are two types of blizzards. The one we think of most is when snow falls from the sky. But a ground blizzard happens when strong winds blow snow that is already on the ground. This makes it hard to see.

A blizzard is a powerful storm. It is a very bad snowstorm. It is not a blizzard just because it is snowing outside. A blizzard must have strong winds. It needs to last for three hours or more. The snow must also make it hard to see.

Wind must be 35 miles per hour (mph) (56 km/h) or greater during a blizzard. Visibility must be 0.25 miles (402 m) or less.

The Storm of the **Century** happened in 1993. Fifty-six inches (142 cm) of snow fell in Tennessee. Records were broken for how cold it was in the South. Ten million houses were left without power. As the name suggests, it really was a once in a lifetime event.

The Storm of the Century caused a lot of snow to fall, but it also caused at least 10 tornadoes.

Blizzards can be huge. They can be miles long. They can cover many states or a whole country. The Storm of the Century covered almost half of the United States in snow. It was such a big storm that

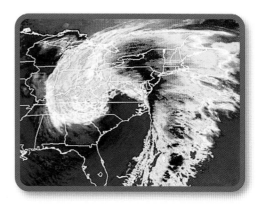

it stretched from Honduras to eastern Canada.

WHAT CAN A BLIZZARD DO?

Collapsed roofs

Power outages

Downed trees

Dangerously cold temperatures

°C °F

50 120
40 100
30 80
20 60
10 40
0 20
10 0
20 20
30

Car accidents

Frozen pipes

Chapter 2

WALKING IN A WINTER WONDERLAND

We all know the Christmas songs. Snow seems magical during the winter holidays. But what happens during a bad blizzard just before Christmas? People living in upstate New York and eastern Canada did not have to guess in December 2013.

Syracuse, New York, is one of the snowiest cities in the world. It gets about 114 inches (290 cm) of snow each year.

Where Do
BLIZZARDS HAPPEN?

BLIZZARD RANGE

2013 New England/
Eastern Canada blizzard

NORTH
AMERICA

EUROPE

ASIA

2022 Buffalo
blizzard

Pacific
Ocean

AFRICA

1993 Storm of
the Century

1996 North
American
blizzard

Pacific
Ocean

SOUTH
AMERICA

Atlantic
Ocean

Indian
Ocean

AUSTRALIA

N

W   E

S

Atlantic
Ocean

ANTARCTICA

Blizzards happen mostly during winter months. Sometimes they happen in fall or spring. On December 19, 2013, a warm front from Texas mixed with the cold air from Canada. This caused a big blizzard and ice storm. It was five days long.

By Christmas Eve, the blizzard was over. Some people were still without power. They wondered how they would celebrate the holiday.

Blizzards are getting stronger. **Climate change** causes more **moisture** in the air. This means more snow will fall. It also means that blizzards can happen more often.

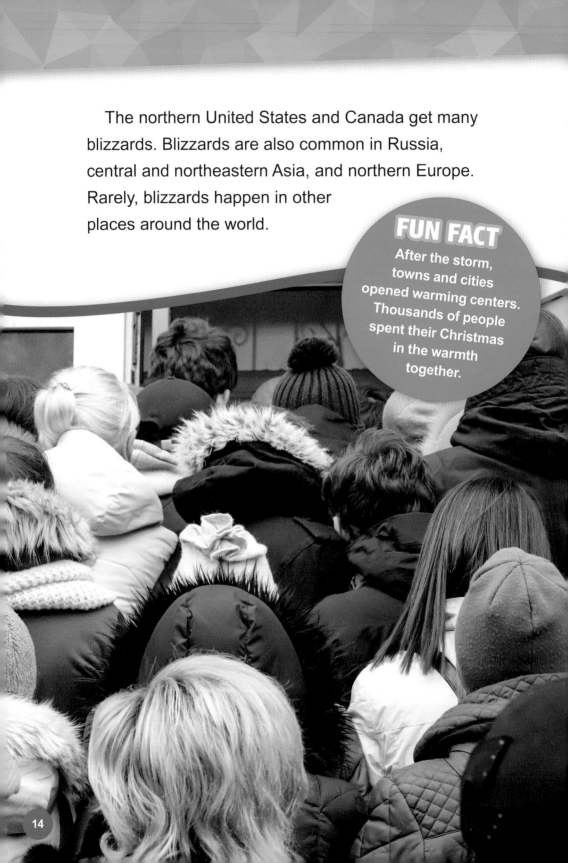

The northern United States and Canada get many blizzards. Blizzards are also common in Russia, central and northeastern Asia, and northern Europe. Rarely, blizzards happen in other places around the world.

FUN FACT

After the storm, towns and cities opened warming centers. Thousands of people spent their Christmas in the warmth together.

CAN IT SNOW IN TEXAS?

Sometimes blizzards happen in warmer locations. It is harder for these places to have this weather. They do not have the supplies to support large snowfalls. In 2021, Texas was hit with a blizzard. It was the most expensive winter storm on record because they were unprepared.

Chapter 3

WARM AND COZY

Some blizzards can lead to other disasters. In January 1996, the North American blizzard made life for Americans on the East Coast pause. Forty-eight inches (122 cm) of snow fell. So much snow that it caused widespread flooding when it melted.

HELPING HANDS

Winter is hard for the homeless. During blizzards, some businesses open for homeless people. They let them spend time indoors away from the cold. Warm food and drinks are also shared.

The Northeast Snowfall Impact Scale measures how bad blizzards get. The North American blizzard of 1996 is one of only three blizzards with the highest ranking.

Supercomputers are used to help track blizzards. Scientists give the computers information. They predict where blizzards will go. They also predict how much snow will fall. Their **forecasts** are correct 85 percent of the time. Though the North American blizzard broke records, that was predicted. It was a classic nor'easter that was made worse by cold air from New York.

Emergency Blizzard Kit

- Flashlight and batteries
- Cell phone and charger
- Candles and matches
- 3-day supply of ready-to-eat food and water per person
- First aid kit and a supply of prescription medicine

It is most important to keep safe and warm during a blizzard. Roads can be hard to drive on. Sometimes they are covered in ice. Snowplows remove snow and **de-ice** roads during a storm. It is safest to stay off the roads.

Blizzards can cause damage. After the blizzard in 1996, President Bill Clinton declared nine states as disaster areas. This is why it is safest to stay inside. It is smart to have a way to keep warm if the power goes out. A fireplace or generator can help.

Blizzards can cause schools to close. They can also cause flight and train cancellations.

Chapter 4

INTO THE UNKNOWN

Sometimes a blizzard is so strong that people start calling it fun names. A huge blizzard hit the eastern United States in December 2022. Buffalo, New York, had the worst of it. Since then, it has been called a "once in a **generation** storm." It has also been called the "Storm of the Century."

BLIZZARD SNOWFALL TOTALS

2022 Buffalo blizzard

4.9 feet
(59 inches)
1.48 meters

1993 Storm of the Century

4.7 feet
(56 inches)
1.42 meters

1996 North American blizzard

4.0 feet
(48 inches)
1.22 meters

**2013 New England/
Eastern Canada blizzard**

1.2 feet
(14 inches)
0.36 meters

6
5
4
3
2
1
0 feet

**AVERAGE MAN
6 feet (72 inches)
1.80 meters**

It can look really pretty after a blizzard. But we still have to keep safe. Don't go out right away. Blizzards can cause trees and power lines to fall. Wait until the roads are cleared.

More than 18,000 flights were cancelled because of the blizzard in the eastern United States. Some people had to find other ways home for Christmas.

CAREFUL KEEPING WARM

Some people try to get warm in their cars when the power goes out. This can be dangerous. This can cause carbon monoxide poisoning if they are still in their garage. Always be careful of your surroundings.

Blizzards can be expensive. Snow and ice are heavy. Winds are strong. This causes damage. About 6.3 million people lost power at some point during the storm in 2022. The Federal Emergency Management Agency (FEMA) helps after natural disasters. They repair expensive damage from storms.

Farah and Ali's dad told them all about blizzards. It started with the story about the blizzard he lived through in 1993, but they had to know more. Blizzards were just so cool!

"I'm so glad we're safe and warm inside," their dad said. "You guys are the best blizzard company."

They watched the snow fall. The power had gone out while their dad told the story. Ali screamed. But the more they learned about blizzards, the better they felt. They built a fire in the fireplace and bundled up in blankets.

"Do you think we can make cookies when the lights come back on?" Ali asked.

"I think blizzard cookies are a perfect idea."

BEYOND THE BOOK

After reading the book, it's time to think about what you learned. Try the following exercises to jump-start your ideas.

THINK

FIND OUT MORE. There are so many blizzards each year. Are you interested in finding out more? Look it up on the web, or check out a book from the library. Maybe even ask someone you know if they've ever experienced a blizzard!

CREATE

ART TIME. Can you draw a blizzard? Look up a picture and grab some markers and paper. How big is your blizzard? Where is it located? The sky is the limit!

SHARE

THE MORE YOU KNOW. Share what you learned about blizzards. Use your own words to write a paragraph. What are the main ideas of this book? What facts from the book can you use to support those ideas? Share your paragraph with a classmate. Do they have any comments or questions?

GROW

HELP OUT! Blizzards can be destructive storms. Find an organization in your area that helps people after disasters. Can you volunteer? Can your family donate to the organization? You can also help by letting people know this organization exists.

RESEARCH NINJA

Visit **www.ninjaresearcher.com/7393** to learn how
to take your research skills and book report writing to the next level!

Research

SEARCH LIKE A PRO
Learn how to use search engines to find useful websites.

FACT OR FAKE
Discover how you can tell a trusted website from an untrustworthy resource.

TEXT DETECTIVE
Explore how to zero in on the information you need most.

SHOW YOUR WORK
Research responsibly—learn how to cite sources.

Write

DOWNLOADABLE BOOK REPORT FORMS

GET TO THE POINT
Learn how to express your main ideas.

PLAN OF ATTACK
Learn prewriting exercises and create an outline.

Further Resources

BOOKS

Johnson, Robin. *What Is a Blizzard?* New York: Crabtree Publishing, 2016.

Meister, Cari. *Disaster Zone: Blizzards*. Minneapolis, MN: Jump!, 2016.

Zoehfeld, Kathleen Weidner. *What Makes a Blizzard?* New York: HarperCollins, 2018.

WEBSITES

FACTSURFER

Factsurfer.com gives you a safe, fun way to find more information.

1. Go to www.factsurfer.com.

2. Enter "Blizzards" into the search box and click 🔍

3. Select your book cover to see a list of related websites.

Glossary

carbon monoxide poisoning: A sickness that happens when breathing in this gas

century: One hundred years

climate change: Shift in weather and temperatures

de-ice: To melt ice

forecast: An educated guess on the weather

generation: People born or living at the same time

moisture: When something feels wet

snowbank: A big pile of snow

supercomputers: Very big computers

visibility: How far you can see

About the Author

Madeline Nixon is an Ontario-based author of *Feathers*, a collection of paranormal short stories, as well as academic articles, and several educational children's books. She works as a writer, editor, and researcher. Madeline loves the snow, exploring places rich in history, and dyeing her hair fun colors.

Index

PHOTO CREDITS

The images in this book are reproduced through the courtesy of: justkgoomm/Shutterstock Images, cover (top); Igor Link/Shutterstock Images, cover (bottom sign); MaLija/Shutterstock Images, cover (backgound); Serge Skiba/ Shutterstock Images, p. 4–5; GryT/Shutterstock Images, p. 5; V_Sot_Visual_Content/Shutterstock Images, p. 6; FLHC 3/Alamy, p. 7, 23; NASA/Wikimedia Commons, p. 7; National Oceanic and Atmospheric Administration/Wikimedia Commons, p. 8; Dennis Harper/Wikimedia Commons, p. 8 (bottom); fotolyubitel/Shutterstock Images, p. 9 (top left); ND700/Shutterstock Images, p. 9 (top right); captainmilos/Shutterstock Images, p. 9 (middle left); Marian Weyo/ Shutterstock Images, p. 9 (middle right); GRADIENT BACKGROUND/Shutterstock Images, p. 9 (bottom left); Danila Shtantsov/Shutterstock Images, p. 9 (bottom right); Sven Hansche/Shutterstock Images, p. 9, 23 (background); Debra Millet/Shutterstock Images, p. 10; US NOAA/Wikimedia Commons, p. 11; Robyn Richardson/Wikimedia Commons, p. 12; ruskpp/Shutterstock Images, p. 13, 23 (3rd photo); rospoint/Shutterstock Images, p. 14; Charlzalan/Shutterstock Images, p. 15; Yuliya Yesina/Wikimedia Commons, p. 16; Drop of Light/Shutterstock Images, p. 17; Leo Morgan/ Shutterstock Images, p. 18; photka/Shutterstock Images, p. 19 (top); Lubo Ivanko/Shutterstock Images, p. 19 (bottom); Samshawv/Wikimedia Commons, p. 20; ssuaphotos Shutterstock Images, p. 21; CreativeAngela/Shutterstock Images, p. 22; Mikhail Leonov/Shutterstock Images, p. 23 (1st photo); Dennis Harper/Wikimedia Commons, p. 23 (2nd photo); Anthony Quintano/Wikimedia Commons, p. 23 (4th photo); PBouman/Shutterstock Images, p. 24 (top); gomoosin/ Shutterstock Images, p. 24 (bottom); frantic00/Shutterstock Images, p. 25; Daniel Llargues/Shutterstock Images, p. 26 (circle); Aaron Skolnik/Wikimedia Commons, p. 26; AlexMaster/Shutterstock Images, p. 27.